Copyright © 2023 by Northwest Gospel Church

Contributers Include: Courtney Huna, Noah Soistmann, Max Janusch, Shelby Larson, Natalie Galloway, Joel Huna, and Mike Clarensau.

You may reproduce, distribute, and transmit this publication with the specific permission of Northwest Gospel Church. For permission requests, write to the address or email address below.

Northwest Gospel Church
305 NE 192nd Ave
Vancouver, WA 98684
info@nwgospel.com

Scripture quotations are from the ESV® Bible (The Holy Bible, English Standard Version®), copyright © 2001 by Crossway. All rights reserved.

Ordering Information:
To order copies of this study guide, contact Northwest Gospel Church at the address or email address listed above.

Philippians:
That We May Know Him
Sermon & Study Guide

Prepared by
Northwest Gospel Church

CONTENTS

How to Use this Study Guide..........7
Welcome to Philippi 9
Philippians 1:1-11..........15
Philippians 1:12-18a 31
Philippians 1:18b-30 45
Philippians 2:1-11 61
Philippians 2:12-18 75
Philippians 2:19-30 91
Philippians 3:1-11..........107
Philippians 3:12-16 123
Philippians 3:17-4:1 137
Philippians 4:2-9 151
Philippians 4:10-13 167
Philippians 4:14-23 181
Closing Reflection 195
Scripture References 199

HOW TO USE THIS STUDY GUIDE

This study guide was written by the leadership of Northwest Gospel Church for the people of Northwest Gospel Church. More specifically, this guide was created to be a resource to NGC's Community Groups.

Our hope for this study is that it equips the church to understand, love, and obey the written Word of God. We know that as we study God's Word together, we will be changed for his glory and our good.

Each week, there will be multiple elements that are designed to help you in your study, both individually and as a group. Don't feel like you are required to complete each element of this book (there won't be a test at the end of this session!), but do use this guide to assist in your study of the book.

Every week contains the following:

> INTRODUCTION: We'll start with a few paragraphs to help you wrap your mind around the biblical text.
>
> THE TEXT: Each week's text is given at the beginning of each week, printed with the permission of Crossway.
>
> SERMON NOTES: Use this space to take notes during Sunday's sermon.
>
> ENGAGE THE TEXT (Five Days): This is for your personal study. These starters will help you engage with the current week's passage, as well as other biblical texts that contain similar subject matter.

JOURNAL: We've created space during each week for you to journal on what you're learning and what God is speaking to you through His Word.

GROUP DISCUSSION QUESTIONS: It is our hope that you will engage this text in the context of a Community Group. These questions are meant to help start discussion as you meet together each week.

GROUP ACTIVITY: Each week, we'll provide a way for your group to engage the text together. Sometimes, this will take the form of a prayer, a video to watch, or simply another outlet for conversation.

YOUR QUESTIONS: We want to encourage you to note any questions that you'd like to discuss with your group. Use this space to make note of those questions.

NOTES FROM GROUP DISCUSSION: Use this space to jot down takeaways from your time together as a group.

Again, our hope is that you grow in your faith over the course of these weeks together, and it is our prayer that this guide assists you in that endeavor. We are praying for you as you engage with God's Word and God's People.

For His Glory,

Tyler Clarenson

Executive Pastor of Ministries

WELCOME TO PHILIPPI

If you walked into the city of Philippi in the early century you would witness a bustling city. Meandering down the streets, you would experience a market full of smells and sounds. Food and goods for sale, an occurrence only resulting from cultures and trades colliding. The diversity of people from vendors, soldiers, magicians, and the poor filling the streets. What unites this city are the rippling bold flags of the Roman Empire. Philippi was "a leading city of the district of Macedonia and a Roman Colony" (Acts 16:12). Here, allegiance to Rome was supreme, and Caesar was worshipped as king and "god."

It's in this context that Paul first arrived to Philippi preaching allegiance to another King, Jesus (Acts 16). The Apostles' were welcomed by the women of the town, including Lydia, seemingly the first convert and one who opened her home to the Apostles. Though Paul and Silas' initial reception was friendly, eventually it ended in a common place for Paul, prison. By the power of the Spirit, Paul freed a young woman from a spirit of divination, thwarting her slave-owners' sinister use of her for profit. In reaction to their threat of livelihood, they started a riot in the city claiming the Apostles were acting unlawful to Roman rule. There in prison, the Lord did what he always does and worked a miracle. Sure, Paul and Silas were miraculously saved from prison, but the real miracle was that, in their detainment, the Roman guard and his whole family came to belief in Christ (Acts 16:31).

This is the beginning of the disciples in Philippi; a merchant woman named Lydia and a Roman soldier. Through these believers, Christ built a church in Philippi, not united under the Roman banner, but under the blood of Christ. It is this church that Paul wrote to years later from another prison. The church had inevitably grown, as Paul writes to the Elders and Deacons of the Philippian church (Philippians 1:1), and it is with great affection,

Philippians: That We May Know Him

love, and joy in the Spirit's work in that church that Paul writes to these believers. Imprisoned for the message of the gospel, Paul exhorts this church to "press on" in knowing Christ, with gospel joy and unity until the great day of seeing Christ face to face.

MESSAGE OF PHILIPPIANS
Press on to know Christ and persevere in Gospel joy and unity until the Day of Christ.

Knowing Christ Leads to Gospel Joy

As a letter written in prison, Philippians is in stark contrast with the circumstances Paul is facing. Above any of Paul's other letters, Philippians speaks strongly about joy and rejoicing. It seems backwards that while Paul is in prison he declares his joy and calls others to joy. Like his first experience in Philippi, Paul recognizes that his present imprisonment is the means of spreading the gospel to the imperial guard and even to Caesar's household (1:12; 4:21). Not only that, his imprisonment is emboldening other believers. This is only possible because Paul's joy is derivative of something else. Paul's joy comes from the supremacy of Christ (2:5-11) and specifically "the surpassing worth of knowing Christ" (3:8). This is what allows Paul to be content in struggle (4:11-13) and to value Christ above his own life (1:21, 3:7). Paul calls fellow believers to join him in his rejoicing and to abandon anxiety through thanksgiving and prayer (4:6).

Knowing Christ Leads to Gospel Unity

Not only does Paul call believers to rejoice no matter their circumstances, but he also calls them to endure in unity. He declares that a life worthy of the gospel is one where believers strive side-by-side together for the gospel (1:27). Meaning, the quality of the message of the gospel is founded on the quality of Christian unity. Paul asks believers to be of the same mind and live in humility toward one another following the example of Christ's humility (2:1-11). He even calls out specific members of the church and exhorts them to be united in the Lord (4:2-3).

Knowing Christ in a Life of Faith

Paul's bold statements such as "to live is Christ, and to die is gain" (2:21) reveals his hope in Christ as he looks forward to "the day of Christ." He divulges that any righteousness he has comes from faith in the Lord who shared his death and resurrection with those who believe (3:9-10). Because Paul has been claimed by Christ, he continues to endure and press on in faith in Christ until the end (3:12-14). Ultimately, Paul is convinced that what the Lord has started He will complete in Paul and in the believers (1:6). Paul endures and looks forward to the day when he will be with Christ who is the object of his joy, unity, and faith.

STRUCTURE

- **Greeting & Intro** (1:1-26): Paul greets the believers in love and affection, grateful for their faith and partnership in the gospel. He then updates them on his situation and the state of gospel ministry happening from others.

- **Unity in Christ** (1:27-2:11): For the sake of the message of the gospel, Paul calls the believers to unity, to be of one mind, to work out conflict, and to humbly treat one another based on the example of Christ's humility. Unity is founded in the gospel; Christ in all his glory humbled himself to die for sinners and is therefore the one whom all creation worships.

- **Living as Lights** (2:12-30): Paul then leans into some practical instructions on what it means to live as Christians and to allow the light of Christ to shine through all that they do. It is revealed in their sanctification, holy living, and eternal perspective.

Philippians: That We May Know Him

- **Perseverance in the Faith** (3:1-4:1): The Philippian Christians experienced as much weariness, doubt, and anxiety as any have in all of history. Yet, Paul reminds them that the Day of Christ is coming, it is worth pressing on, and they can rejoice in Christ even in their present suffering.

- **Final Encouragement & Greetings** (4:2-23): Paul once again calls for unity among certain believers and reminds them of the Lord's provision and care of them.

THEMES:

- **Gospel**[1] - The gospel takes center stage in Philippians. All of Paul's exhortation will come out the centrality of what Jesus has done on the cross.

- **Life & Faith**[2] - Coming out of the centrality of the gospel, on several occasions, Paul declares that it is for Christ that he lives his entire life, and if he is to lose his life for the gospel, then it is gain.

- **Salvation**[3] - Paul has a brief but complete outline of salvation in this epistle. He encourages the believers that their salvation will be made complete in Christ. However, believers are to also work out their salvation while they press on until the Day of Christ.

- **Unity**[4] - Multiple times Paul calls believers to be of one mind, but his reasoning is the same for all his other exhortations; because of Christ. Believers are to follow the example of Christ's humility and unite in their witness of him.

---

[1] Philippians 1:5, 7, 12, 14, 16, 27; 2:22, 30; 4:3, 15
[2] Philippians 1:20-22; 3:7-8
[3] Philippians 1:6; 2:12-13; 3:12
[4] Philippians 1:27, 11; 2:2-5; 4:2

Welcome To Philippi

- **Glory**[5] - In this letter, Paul's eyes are on the glory of Christ. It is for this reason that he does anything, and it is the reason that Paul exhorts the believers.

- **Suffering**[6] - Paul is not shy about his suffering in this book, and yet he has found joy and contentment because his hope is rooted in Christ and not in his circumstances.

- **Joy / Rejoicing**[7] - As previously mentioned, one of Paul's main exhortations to the church in Philippi is to rejoice!

---

[5]Philippians 1:26, 11; 2:11; 3:3, 19; 4:19
[6]Philippians 1:29; 2:27; 3:8, 10; 4:12
[7]Philippians 1:4, 18, 25; 2:2, 17, 18, 28, 29; 3:1; 4:1, 4, 10

PHILIPPIANS 1:1-11

Introduction

The development of technology in this age has seemingly shrunk the world. We have an interconnectedness across the globe that we've never had before. It facilitates long distance relationships and connections over distances that, not too long ago, would have separated people forever. Even so, we feel the sting of loved ones being far away, in different time zones, and no longer sharing in our everyday moments. Feelings of longing and affection grow as we desire to know how our loved ones are doing.

In the First Century, the world was certainly not as connected as it is today and a distance of only ten miles could even create great disconnect between people. Paul writes this letter to the Philippians likely while he is in jail in Rome, over 800 miles from the church in Philippi. The relationships that he made there, new believers he saw come to faith, and his dear friends, he will all likely never see again. It's with great love, affection, longing, and eagerness that he writes to this growing church. He is filled with joy remembering their love for the Lord and their work in the gospel and he has full faith that the Lord is continuing to work in them and will continue to work in them until the completion of days. With that same joy he sends a prayer for the church that they would grow in love, wisdom, discernment, good works, and effectiveness in gospel work.

As we see in the whole of this letter, Paul has reasons to be sad but ultimately has a reason to rejoice. In this case, Paul could grieve about being removed from brothers and sisters in Christ, but his confidence in Christ Jesus gives him a sure faith that at the very least, he will see these dear friends again on the Day of Jesus Christ.

Philippians: That We May Know Him

The Day of Jesus Christ is a day that we also look forward to with hope. Not only for the completion of our walk in this life and for the fulfilled righteousness of the Lord, but also for a similar reason as Paul. One day, all those in Christ will stand together before the throne and generations of faithful men and women will rejoice together forever in Jesus who has saved us. What a day that will be!

PHILIPPIANS 1:1-11

[1] Paul and Timothy, servants of Christ Jesus,
To all the saints in Christ Jesus who are at Philippi, with the overseers and deacons:
[2] Grace to you and peace from God our Father and the Lord Jesus Christ.

Thanksgiving and Prayer
[3] I thank my God in all my remembrance of you, [4] always in every prayer of mine for you all making my prayer with joy, [5] because of your partnership in the gospel from the first day until now. [6] And I am sure of this, that he who began a good work in you will bring it to completion at the day of Jesus Christ. [7] It is right for me to feel this way about you all, because I hold you in my heart, for you are all partakers with me of grace, both in my imprisonment and in the defense and confirmation of the gospel. [8] For God is my witness, how I yearn for you all with the affection of Christ Jesus. [9] And it is my prayer that your love may abound more and more, with knowledge and all discernment, [10] so that you may approve what is excellent, and so be pure and blameless for the day of Christ, [11] filled with the fruit of righteousness that comes through Jesus Christ, to the glory and praise of God.

Philippians: That We May Know Him

SERMON NOTES

Philippians 1:1-11

Philippians: That We May Know Him

DAY 1: ENGAGE THE TEXT

Read: Acts 16:1-15. Who is Timothy and how did Paul come to do ministry with him? What background does this give us about the letter to the Philippians?

DAY 2: ENGAGE THE TEXT

Read: Acts 16:16-40 How did the gospel first come to Philippi? How does the background from Acts give us greater insight to Paul's opening words to the letter to the Philippians?

DAY 3: ENGAGE THE TEXT

Read this week's passage again and circle/underline terms like "gospel," "joy," "love," and "prayer." How are these themes connected? What could the Lord be teaching you through this connection?

DAY 4: ENGAGE THE TEXT

Read: 1 Thessalonians 5:1–11; 2 Peter 3:10–13 & Revelation 20:11–21:8. What is "The Day of Christ" and what happens on that day? What is Paul's confidence as he waits for that day?

Philippians: That We May Know Him

DAY 5: ENGAGE THE TEXT

Re-Read: Philippians 1:9. What does Paul pray the believers would abound/increase in? What is the result of that thing increasing in their life? What would this look like in your life?

_____
_____
_____
_____
_____
_____
_____
_____
_____
_____
_____
_____
_____
_____
_____
_____
_____
_____
_____
_____
_____

JOURNAL QUESTION

Each of us could probably create a never ending list of things we want to grow in or change about ourselves to be an overall "better person." Even in this passage, we see things like abounding love and righteousness showing us our lack in those areas. However, Philippians 1:6 shines out reminding us that we are not even sovereign in our own righteousness; it is a work that Jesus is ACTIVELY doing in us.

How do you see the hand of Jesus working in your life right now? Where is he chiseling away sin? Where is he bringing the comfort of the gospel? Pray for these things and that you will lean into the Spirit's work in your heart.

Philippians: That We May Know Him

Philippians 1:1-11

GROUP DISCUSSION QUESTIONS

1. How would you describe Paul's tone in the opening lines of this letter? How does he feel about this church?

2. How does Paul's attitude toward the church inform us about a pastor's heart for their church? Have you seen this modeled? How does this confront your own feelings towards the church?

3. Paul prays for the church's love and righteousness to grow in Christ. What is the goal of the increase of love and righteousness? What then is the purpose of the church and the community of believers?

4. How would you say you're doing with affection for other believers? How can you pray that the Lord would increase your heart in love for others?

5. Philippians is a letter full of some of the most well-known Bible passages, starting here in verse 6. How does this passage bring us hope? Where in your life is it hard for you to believe this? Feel free to refer to your response in this week's Big Picture Journal Question.

GROUP ELEMENT

In Philippians 1:9-11, Paul is praying for this growing church to grow in love, discernment, and righteousness. Take a moment to read this passage and pray this over our church and families

OTHER RESOURCES

As we begin this series in Philippians it's always great to get an overview from the excellent work from the Bible Project. You can check out their Philippians video an all extra resources at nwgospel.com/philippiansresources.

HAVE A QUESTION?

GROUP DISCUSSION NOTES

PHILIPPIANS 1:12-18A
Introduction

Perspective can make or break many situations. A particular line of sight around a bush at an intersection can impact your decision to stall or accelerate into traffic. Decisions at work or in leadership depend on the quality of information you have at hand. Knowing the full truth and context of a situation determines successful mediation between children, friends, or family in conflict. There is a negative correlation between knowledge of a situation and your level of anxiety; the more you know, the less you worry.

As we read Paul's letter here to the Philippians, it could easily feel like Paul knows something we don't. He is facing imprisonment without knowing the outcome. He's facing opposition from those who ought to call him brothers, and he is far from those he loves. All things considered, if we were in the same boat I'm not sure we would say, "I rejoice!" What can Paul see that we can't? As we discussed last week, Paul has his eyes on a much later date. He's not just thinking about his present circumstances, but he has his eyes on "the Day of Jesus Christ" (1:6). Yet, in his present circumstances, he also has his eyes on the mission. Paul cares less about what he is feeling and chooses to look where the gospel is impacting. Those who imprisoned him are hearing the gospel. A whole new frontier for mission work has opened up in the imperial guard. Even those who oppose him are proclaiming Christ. The name of Christ being made known is far more important than Paul's name being cursed or acquitted.

When we look at the work of our hands and the days before us, it's easy to lose sight of these two things; gospel work and the hope of eternity. It is both a discipline and an act of grace to be able to look up from our "today" and see where the Lord is working. May he give us those eyes today and may it fill us with joy to see and know Christ's work in and through us right now.

PHILIPPIANS 1:12-18A

The Advance of the Gospel

[12] I want you to know, brothers, that what has happened to me has really served to advance the gospel, [13] so that it has become known throughout the whole imperial guard and to all the rest that my imprisonment is for Christ. [14] And most of the brothers, having become confident in the Lord by my imprisonment, are much more bold to speak the word without fear.

[15] Some indeed preach Christ from envy and rivalry, but others from good will. [16] The latter do it out of love, knowing that I am put here for the defense of the gospel. [17] The former proclaim Christ out of selfish ambition, not sincerely but thinking to afflict me in my imprisonment. [18] What then? Only that in every way, whether in pretense or in truth, Christ is proclaimed, and in that I rejoice.

Philippians 1:12-18a

SERMON NOTES

Philippians: That We May Know Him

Philippians 1:12-18a

DAY 1: ENGAGE THE TEXT

Re-Read: Acts 16:25-24. How has Paul already seen gospel fruit come from imprisonment? What gospel fruit is he experiencing now?

Philippians: That We May Know Him

DAY 2: ENGAGE THE TEXT

How does Paul live out James 2:2? How does Paul see his trial as meaningful work for Christ and not a delay or hindrance to his mission?

Philippians 1:12-18a

DAY 3: ENGAGE THE TEXT

Read: Acts 4:23-31 and 28:30-31. From the beginning, the church was marked by gospel boldness and Paul lived it out from his conversion onward. Where does the believer's source of boldness come from? What hope could be stronger than current threats of violence and death?

Philippians: That We May Know Him

DAY 4: ENGAGE THE TEXT

Continue from last week and circle/underline words like "gospel," "rejoice," "love," etc. How does Paul's purpose continue to unfold? What is Paul's motivation? How can we be more aware of uniting in the same purpose?

DAY 5: ENGAGE THE TEXT

Read: 2 Corinthians 11:1-15. Paul often experienced conflict with other preachers of the gospel, some who just wanted to injure him like those he mentions in Philippians and others who were false teachers. Compare what Paul says in Philippians 1:12-18 to what he says in 2 Corinthians 11. How are the situations similar and different? Does Paul's motivation or mission change?

Philippians: That We May Know Him

JOURNAL QUESTION

Paul had a heaven-ward and eternal perspective on the sufferings he faced in his life. With eyes on Jesus and on the promise of knowing and seeing Jesus more and more, Paul was able to rejoice and view his circumstances with new eyes. What struggles are you facing today that seem to blur your view of Jesus? How can you look past or through those things to see Jesus and have an eternal perspective? How does this change your view of your present struggles?

Philippians 1:12-18a

Philippians: That We May Know Him

GROUP DISCUSSION QUESTIONS

1. Paul is experiencing gospel fruit even while he is seemingly "useless" in prison. What does this show us about the mission of Christ and the power of the gospel? What encouragement or challenge does this give to your current season of life?

2. Paul's experience in prison and the work of God through his circumstances naturally gave other believers encouragement to proclaim the gospel boldly. Whose witness, story, or testimony encourages you to continue in the faith and proclaim the gospel boldly?

3. What is Paul's attitude toward those who proclaim the gospel but are opposed to him? Have you encountered a similar situation before? How did/can you respond in circumstances like this?

4. Who could the Lord be reaching through your present struggle or trial? How might the Lord have you right where you need to be for his mission and the advance of the gospel?

GROUP ELEMENT

What Paul experienced is still common today, Christians around the world are in prison for their faith in Christ. Take a moment as a group to pray for imprisoned and persecuted Christians. You can choose to pray for Christians in a country from the World Watch List in this week's resources.

OTHER RESOURCES

Open Doors Ministry lists the top 50 countries where it is most dangerous to be a Christian. You can see that resource and all others for this series at nwgospel.com/philippiansresources.

HAVE A QUESTION?

GROUP DISCUSSION NOTES

PHILIPPIANS 1:18B-30
Introduction

Remember this moment as a kid: It's summer and the temperature is rising to the level of "why would I be outside right now." It's the middle of the day, the time where the air is still and stale and it seems like nothing is happening. You're "BORED!" But then you hear it. In the distance, a faint chime catches in the air. It's the song that no one knows the name of, but it has a universal meaning; the ice cream truck! You have seconds, maybe minutes if you're lucky, to not only find some spare change in the couch but to convince your parent(s) to "just this once!" let you get something from the ice cream truck. You search for the right words, but in desperation you blurt out, "if I don't get some I will DIE!"

As adults now, and maybe with children of your own playing out that scene, you find yourself rolling your eyes. It's hyperbole. No one will die from lack of ice cream. However, as we get older, the feeling still exists in our life, but it just looks more mature. We have careers, reputations, relationships, hobbies, pets, possessions, and a whole host of anything under the sun that we'd shout, "if I lose this I will DIE!" From the petty to the deeply valuable, as humans we have a tendency to hold a number of created things as supreme in our heart while forgetting the Creator who gave them to us.

Paul's letter to the Philippians confronts us with this truth as he declares that in life or death there is only one thing that matters: Jesus Christ. If Paul lives, it will be for Christ. If he dies, it will be for Christ whom he will meet face to face. Nothing else is more supreme. We find this tension in our soul as we wish to declare the same but also have many "loves" that are not Christ. However, knowing and loving Christ at this level is the only antidote for suffering and source of eternal joy.

Philippians: That We May Know Him

As the Word shows us the things that we are prone to love more than Christ, may his Spirit transform our hearts to center around Christ alone. May we experience this same confidence and joy that Paul has in the Christ who has saved us and given us eternal life.

Prone to wander, Lord I feel it
Prone to leave the God I love
Here's my heart, oh take and seal it
Seal it for Thy courts above[1]

---

[1] "Come, Thou Fount of Every Blessing" written by Thomas, J. H.

PHILIPPIANS 1:18B-30

To Live Is Christ
Yes, and I will rejoice, [19] for I know that through your prayers and the help of the Spirit of Jesus Christ this will turn out for my deliverance, [20] as it is my eager expectation and hope that I will not be at all ashamed, but that with full courage now as always Christ will be honored in my body, whether by life or by death. [21] For to me to live is Christ, and to die is gain. [22] If I am to live in the flesh, that means fruitful labor for me. Yet which I shall choose I cannot tell. [23] I am hard pressed between the two. My desire is to depart and be with Christ, for that is far better. [24] But to remain in the flesh is more necessary on your account. [25] Convinced of this, I know that I will remain and continue with you all, for your progress and joy in the faith, [26] so that in me you may have ample cause to glory in Christ Jesus, because of my coming to you again.

[27] Only let your manner of life be worthy of the gospel of Christ, so that whether I come and see you or am absent, I may hear of you that you are standing firm in one spirit, with one mind striving side by side for the faith of the gospel, [28] and not frightened in anything by your opponents. This is a clear sign to them of their destruction, but of your salvation, and that from God. [29] For it has been granted to you that for the sake of Christ you should not only believe in him but also suffer for his sake, [30] engaged in the same conflict that you saw I had and now hear that I still have.

Philippians: That We May Know Him

SERMON NOTES

Philippians 1:18b-30

Philippians: That We May Know Him

DAY 1: ENGAGE THE TEXT

Read: Romans 1:1-16. In both Romans and in this weeks' passage in Philippians, Paul declares that he is not ashamed of the gospel of Christ. Compare these two passages. Why can Paul declare that he is not ashamed?

Philippians 1:18b-30

DAY 2: ENGAGE THE TEXT

Continue the pattern from previous weeks; circling/underlining words like "gospel," "joy," "glory," etc. How does this connect to Paul's purpose in life or death?

Philippians: That We May Know Him

DAY 3: ENGAGE THE TEXT

Read: Galatians 2:20. How does Paul see the purpose of his life lived in the flesh? Why could Paul be looking forward to death? How do you view life and death?

DAY 4: ENGAGE THE TEXT

Read: Romans 15:1-7 & Ephesians 4:1-6. According to Paul, living a life "worthy of the gospel of Christ" (1:27) is directly connected to our unity in Christ. Compare what Paul says in Romans about how our unity impacts the "volume" of our gospel message in the world. Where are places of disunity in your life that "mute" your gospel witness?

DAY 5: ENGAGE THE TEXT

Read: 1 Peter 4:12-19. What is the Christian view of suffering? Compare your response to trials with to how the Bible instructs us. What do you need to change in your heart and perspective to be in line with his word?

Philippians 1:18b-30

JOURNAL QUESTION

As mentioned in the first week, Philippians is full of well-known passages and we enounter across another one this week in 1:21. Paul says that Life = Christ, therefore death is nothing but a chance to see Christ. If we were to write this equation for ourselves; life = _____, what would we fill in the blank? What, if we lost it today, would feel like death in our lives? Confess these things to the Lord and pray that you can boldly say along with Paul that Life = Christ!

Philippians: That We May Know Him

Philippians 1:18b-30

GROUP DISCUSSION QUESTIONS

1. In verse 19, we see an interesting partnership between the prayers of the church and the Spirit of Jesus. Discuss this partnership and the impact of prayer. How can this passage encourage us in our prayers this week?

2. In verse 20, Paul states that he will not be ashamed of living for Christ. When it comes to living boldly for Christ and communicating the gospel, do you ever feel ashamed? Where do you need Christ's courage today?

3. Paul seems to be anticipating his death; however, it is not motivated by his suffering. Compare the difference between looking forward to seeing Christ and simply escaping this life. Take note to pray for those who particularly need hope in Christ and this perspective change.

4. God's people seem to be marked by a peace that doesn't give way to fear in suffering, and it is a witness to the world. What fears get in the way of your peace in Christ being a clear declaration of your salvation to the world?

5. Paul encourages the church of Philippi to strive side-by-side for the faith of the gospel. Who do you currently have by your side encouraging you to strive for the faith of the gospel? How can we grow as a church in gospel unity?

GROUP ELEMENT

It could be easy to read these passage and conclude that we just need to brush off suffering and grief. However, suffering and grief are real, powerful, and consuming experiences. Take time to list those who need prayer for suffering. Pray for the power of the Spirit to secure them despite the waves of grief. Write these names/needs on cards, paper, notes, etc. and pick one to pray for each week you gather.

OTHER RESOURCES

The parenting resource Risen Motherhood has compiled a list of excellent resources for suffering and grief for a variety of experiences, ages, and not exclusive to mothers or parents. Check out this collection and all our resources at nwgospel.com/philippiansresources.

HAVE A QUESTION?

Philippians 1:18b-30

GROUP DISCUSSION NOTES

PHILIPPIANS 2:1-11
Introduction

If there is a hall of fame for most mind-blowing, life-transforming, and perspective-shifting Bible verses, this passage would absolutely be featured there.

Jesus was perfectly and completely God and man in one person. His life, therefore, perfectly displays for us not just how we can be more like God, but how we can thrive as human beings the way God intended it to be. When we observe and put into practice the principles of this passage, life as a human just seems to make so much more sense. The church is called to be united in mission for the Gospel and affection for Christ. Our lives are not our own. Our relationships are not for selfish gain. We model our life and our relationships the same way Jesus did, with an overabundance of humility and selflessness.

God wants his people to be unified, and now more than ever in our current context it seems like we can find a million petty reasons to be divided even in the church. This passage will challenge our worldly loves, preferences, and opinions. Will we rise to the occasion?

PHILIPPIANS 2:1-11

Christ's Example of Humility

[1] So if there is any encouragement in Christ, any comfort from love, any participation in the Spirit, any affection and sympathy, [2] complete my joy by being of the same mind, having the same love, being in full accord and of one mind. [3] Do nothing from selfish ambition or conceit, but in humility count others more significant than yourselves. [4] Let each of you look not only to his own interests, but also to the interests of others. [5] Have this mind among yourselves, which is yours in Christ Jesus, [6] who, though he was in the form of God, did not count equality with God a thing to be grasped, [7] but emptied himself, by taking the form of a servant, being born in the likeness of men. [8] And being found in human form, he humbled himself by becoming obedient to the point of death, even death on a cross. [9] Therefore God has highly exalted him and bestowed on him the name that is above every name, [10] so that at the name of Jesus every knee should bow, in heaven and on earth and under the earth, [11] and every tongue confess that Jesus Christ is Lord, to the glory of God the Father.

Philippians 2:1-11

SERMON NOTES

Philippians: That We May Know Him

Philippians 2:1-11

DAY 1: ENGAGE THE TEXT

Read: Colossians 3:1-17. How does Colossians give us a bigger picture of the unity that Paul is calling for? What is the reason for our unity, forgiveness, and humility?

Philippians: That We May Know Him

DAY 2: ENGAGE THE TEXT

Read: Colossians 1:15-20 & John 1:1-4. Who is Jesus? Write out some descriptions for him. What then did Jesus "empty himself" of and why is this such radical humility?

DAY 3: ENGAGE THE TEXT

Read: Romans 12:9-21. Compare how Romans and Philippians talk about what it means to love others. What aspects come easy for you and what aspects are hard?

Philippians: That We May Know Him

DAY 4: ENGAGE THE TEXT

Read: Isaiah 42:1-9. How does Jesus embody both the qualities of the promised servant and of the mighty God? What does it mean that Jesus became a servant? How does it compare with our humility?

Philippians 2:1-11

DAY 5: ENGAGE THE TEXT

Read: Revelation 5. One day all of creation will bow the knee to only Jesus. What areas of your life do you find difficult to bow the knee to Jesus? Take a moment to remind yourself of the goodness and greatness of God

JOURNAL QUESTION

This passage is both a beautiful picture of Jesus' love for us as well as a strong call for us to lay down ourselves in love for others. This is probably the hardest thing we will ever do in life, and our pride is the most difficult to overcome. What areas in your life are you most tempted by the sin of selfishness? How can you actively practice humility and selflessness towards others, even when there are disagreements or differing perspectives? Who can you "count more significantly than yourself" this week?

Remember that this mindset "is yours in Christ Jesus" (2:5). Close your time praying that Jesus would change your heart and mind to be more like his.

Philippians 2:1-11

Philippians: That We May Know Him

GROUP DISCUSSION QUESTIONS

1. Read Philippians 2:1-11 together as a group. What words, phrases, exhortations, and encouragements stand out to you?

2. What do you find most challenging about the call to do nothing from selfish ambition?

3. In Philippians 2:6-7, Paul describes Jesus' willingness to empty Himself and take the form of a servant. What does that mean? What is the significance of Jesus' humbling?

4. Verses 3-4 encourage us to consider others as more significant than ourselves. Who in your life has lived out this selfless attitude like Christ towards you? How did their life impact you?

5. This passage ends with a powerful truth, the reality that every knee will bow and every tongue confess Jesus as Lord. What does this declaration mean for us? How can it influence our daily worship and devotion to Christ?

GROUP ELEMENT

"All Hail King Jesus" is a song that we sing often when we gather on Sunday mornings. This song portrays the humiliation and then exaltation of Jesus while he served with us just like the text shares. Take a second to listen to this song and read along to the lyrics.

OTHER RESOURCES

For links to the song "All Hail King Jesus" and all the resources for this series, check out nwgospel.com/philippiansresources.

HAVE A QUESTION?

GROUP DISCUSSION NOTES

PHILIPPIANS 2:12-18
Introduction

Have you ever tried to completely black out a room? Maybe you've attempted to create the ideal in-home theater. Or maybe you've had a fussy infant and you're praying perfect darkness may earn you a few more "zzz's." Or maybe you're the fussy sleeper or a night-shift worker and those new blackout curtains will solve everything. If you've ever attempted a perfectly blacked out space, you know that even the smallest light can seem so bright! You think you've got it all until your eyes adjust and you see the tiny blue indicator light that tells you the fan is on or the alarm clock suddenly seems as bright as the sun. Then once you think you've electrical taped every scrap of light in your room, you see a blaring spotlight from the ceiling reminding you that you have a smoke detector. In the darkest spaces, even the smallest and seemingly most insignificant lights are bright as day.

This is similar to how Paul describes the people of God in a "crooked and twisted generation" (2:15). More specifically, a people who are known for their righteousness in Christ. In a dark world bent toward sin and living for selfish desires, the holiness of God's people shine out as a light into the world. This can seem like a major irritation for those who love and long to live in the dark. Paul himself experienced the trials and persecution of people who would try to stamp out the light. But much like the work of the tired parent, not even the best attempts can completely black out the light. However, there is also a warning in this passage; we can dull our own lights. Paul says that something as simple as grumbling and arguing can damper the bright light of the gospel in our lives. Paul calls believers to unity so that together our lights can show the beauty of Christ in the world as our voices unite in rejoicing in the God who saved us.

Philippians: That We May Know Him

This week, even when it's uncomfortable, allow God's word to reveal the places of grumbling and arguing in your heart. Pray that the Lord will give you contentment and love for the life and people that he's given you.

PHILIPPIANS 2:12-18

Lights in the World

[12] Therefore, my beloved, as you have always obeyed, so now, not only as in my presence but much more in my absence, work out your own salvation with fear and trembling, [13] for it is God who works in you, both to will and to work for his good pleasure.

[14] Do all things without grumbling or disputing, [15] that you may be blameless and innocent, children of God without blemish in the midst of a crooked and twisted generation, among whom you shine as lights in the world, [16] holding fast to the word of life, so that in the day of Christ I may be proud that I did not run in vain or labor in vain. [17] Even if I am to be poured out as a drink offering upon the sacrificial offering of your faith, I am glad and rejoice with you all. [18] Likewise you also should be glad and rejoice with me.

Philippians: That We May Know Him

SERMON NOTES

Philippians 2:12-18

Philippians: That We May Know Him

DAY 1: ENGAGE THE TEXT

Read: Hebrews 13. What are the similarities in Philippians and Hebrews? What is the role of spiritual leaders? How are believers meant to live out/"work out" their salvation?

Philippians 2:12-18

DAY 2: ENGAGE THE TEXT

Read: 1 Peter 2:13-24. How does godly living and our conduct in suffering display the gospel in our lives? What message does your life share right now?

Philippians: That We May Know Him

DAY 3: ENGAGE THE TEXT

Re-read: Philippians 1:6. How does Paul give assurance that the Lord is at work in those who proclaim Christ as Lord? What parts of your life to you need to entrust to the Lord today?

Philippians 2:12-18

DAY 4: ENGAGE THE TEXT

Read: Matthew 5:1-16 & John 8:12-30. How do God's people shine as lights in the world? What does it mean for us to be the light of the world and how do we reflect THE Light of the World?

Philippians: That We May Know Him

DAY 5: ENGAGE THE TEXT

Read: John 6:60-71. The early disciples realized that following Jesus would be difficult. What did the twelve believe that the others didn't? What does it mean to "hold fast to the word of life" (Philippians 2:16)?

Philippians 2:12-18

JOURNAL QUESTION

There is a connection between following Jesus and obeying Jesus. We see this elsewhere in the Bible as well (for example: Matthew 28:19-20; 1 John 5:1-5). How do you respond when you hear the command to obey Jesus? Where is it hardest for you to obey? What part of your sanctification could Jesus be working on in you right now?

Philippians: That We May Know Him

Philippians 2:12-18

GROUP DISCUSSION QUESTIONS

1. In verses 12-13, we once again we see this fascinating partnership between the work of Christ and our work. How do these work together? How do we work out our salvation as Christ works it in us?

2. How do the people of Christ "shine as lights in the world?" What kinds of things (behaviors, attitudes, habits) mark the people of God?

3. Paul exhorts believers to do ALL things without grumbling or disputing. What are the common "grumble-points" for you in your life? What is happening in your heart in those moments?

4. How does our lack of grumbling create a distinct identity of the people of God from the world? Have you seen examples of this in people you know?

5. What does it look like to "hold fast to the word of life?" How does this play out in the daily things that you encounter; work relationships, family, TV/entertainment, etc?

GROUP ELEMENT

"Holding fast to the word" requires knowing and being reminded of God's word. Take some time at the end of your group meeting to find and share some of your favorite passages with one another. You can go around a circle or "popcorn" around, the goal is just to read scripture and encourage one another.

OTHER RESOURCES

For a resource on the significance of the "Day of Christ", check out the video from The Bible Project on "The Day of the Lord" as well as all other series resources at nwgospel.com/philippiansresources.

HAVE A QUESTION?

Philippians 2:12-18

GROUP DISCUSSION NOTES

PHILIPPIANS 2:19-30

Introduction

Who doesn't appreciate a good example? Anyone faced with an important or complicated task can see the value in an example. Elementary-age kids are given examples of good handwriting as they learn. Parents show teenagers how to parallel park before turning them loose on the streets of Clark County. Manufacturers print comical diagrams on large boxes to ensure safe transportation and delivery.

In Philippians 2:19-30, the Apostle Paul offers two good examples for us. After reveling in the humility of Christ (Philippians 2:1-11) and the implications of this humility on the Christian life (Philippians 2:12-18), Paul now presents Timothy and Epaphroditus, two of his gospel co-workers, as examples of service and humility that the Philippians ought to emulate.

Timothy has proven himself as a reliable co-laborer, worker, and follower of Jesus. Epaphroditus has come close to death in his service and love for the Lord. Paul is anxious to send both men to the Philippians as examples of Christ-like humility and service, and as caring workers who will do their part in seeing the gospel grow in breadth and depth.

In calling the Philippians to Christ-like humility, Paul offers two exceptional examples that these Christians ought to imitate. Although we are living two-thousand years later, we too can appreciate and follow the examples held up in God's Word.

PHILIPPIANS 2:19-30

Timothy and Epaphroditus

[19] I hope in the Lord Jesus to send Timothy to you soon, so that I too may be cheered by news of you. [20] For I have no one like him, who will be genuinely concerned for your welfare. [21] For they all seek their own interests, not those of Jesus Christ. [22] But you know Timothy's proven worth, how as a son with a father he has served with me in the gospel. [23] I hope therefore to send him just as soon as I see how it will go with me, [24] and I trust in the Lord that shortly I myself will come also.

[25] I have thought it necessary to send to you Epaphroditus my brother and fellow worker and fellow soldier, and your messenger and minister to my need, [26] for he has been longing for you all and has been distressed because you heard that he was ill. [27] Indeed he was ill, near to death. But God had mercy on him, and not only on him but on me also, lest I should have sorrow upon sorrow. [28] I am the more eager to send him, therefore, that you may rejoice at seeing him again, and that I may be less anxious. [29] So receive him in the Lord with all joy, and honor such men, [30] for he nearly died for the work of Christ, risking his life to complete what was lacking in your service to me.

Philippians 2:19-30

SERMON NOTES

Philippians: That We May Know Him

Philippians 2:19-30

DAY 1: ENGAGE THE TEXT

How does Paul describe Timothy and Epaphroditus? How do these qualities teach you about what God values in his gospel-workers?

DAY 2: ENGAGE THE TEXT

Read: 2 Timothy 1:1-14. Describe the relationship between Paul and Timothy and the ministry they did together. Who is someone that you have looked to as an example of Christ? Who is someone you are/want to set an example for?

Philippians 2:19-30

DAY 3: ENGAGE THE TEXT

Read: 1 Timothy 3:1-13. How do Timothy and Epaphroditus display characters of godly church leadership? How do they present a fuller picture of what Paul wants the Philippians to imitate?

Philippians: That We May Know Him

DAY 4: ENGAGE THE TEXT

Read: Ephesians 6:21-24 & Colossians 4:7-18. According to these verses, what's in it for Paul in sending gospel workers? What do these passages teach us about the two-way blessing of sending out and going on gospel mission?

_____
_____
_____
_____
_____
_____
_____
_____
_____
_____
_____
_____
_____
_____
_____
_____
_____

Philippians 2:19-30

DAY 5: ENGAGE THE TEXT

Read: 1 Thessalonians 5:12-28. Describe how the church family is meant to function together. What is the role and treatment of leadership meant to be like? How are we called to treat one another? What aspects of this confronts attitudes in your heart?

JOURNAL QUESTION

In your life, where are opportunities for you to cultivate humility and service more intentionally? What relationships, situations, spheres of influence, etc. offer you the chance to follow the example of Timothy and Epaphroditus—and ultimately, Christ—in humility and service?

Philippians 2:19-30

Philippians: That We May Know Him

GROUP DISCUSSION QUESTIONS

1. Have you experienced saying goodbye to a pastor, leader, or friend who moved to do gospel work in another part of the country or world? How did you respond to that? How does Paul's attitude in sending off Timothy teach us how to steward these moments and relationships?

2. It seems like these gospel workers lived with a fluid and flexible hold on their life and plans. When we think of following that example, it can create much anxiety in our hearts. What currently prevents you from living with that kind of flexibility of life and plans?

3. Epaphroditus was not a gospel worker by trade, he was a soldier, yet he lived a radically mission-minded, gospel-motivated life. Most of us aren't gospel workers by vocation, yet we are all called to be gospel workers. Where is God calling you to be on mission today?

4. Where are areas that you struggle to model the humility and service of Timothy and Epaphroditus? What encouragement and/or instruction does God offer you in his Word to grow in this part of your Christian life?

5. Why would Paul and, ultimately, the Holy Spirit, decide to include the examples of Timothy and Epaphroditus? How do their examples in addition to the example of Jesus (Philippians 2:1-11) give you a fuller picture of what Christian humility and service should look like?

Philippians 2:19-30

GROUP ELEMENT

Pray this Puritan prayer of repentance together:

Mighty God,
I humble myself for faculties misused,
opportunities neglected,
words ill-advised,
I repent of my folly and inconsiderate ways,
my broken resolutions, untrue service,
my backsliding steps,
my vain thoughts.
O bury my sins in the ocean of Jesus' blood
and let no evil result from my fretful temper,
unseemly behavior, provoking pettiness.
If by unkindness I have wounded or hurt another,
do thou pour in the balm of heavenly consolation;
If I have turned coldly from need, misery, grief,
do not in just anger forsake me:
If I have withheld relief from penury and pain,
do not withhold thy gracious bounty from me.
If I have shunned those who have offended me,
keep open the door of thy heart to my need.

Fill me with an over-flowing ocean of compassion,
the reign of love my motive,
the law of love my rule.

O thou God of all grace, make me more thankful, more humble;
Inspire me with a deep sense of my unworthiness arising from
the depravity of my nature, my omitted duties
my unimproved advantages, thy commands violated by
me.

With all my calls to gratitude and joy
    may I remember that I have reason for sorrow and
    humiliation;
O give me repentance unto life;
Cement my oneness with my blessed Lord,
    that faith may adhere to him more immovably,
    that love may entwine itself round him more tightly,
    that his Spirit may pervade every fiber of my being.
Then send me out to make him known to my fellow-men.[1]

OTHER RESOURCES

For a link to the resource referenced above and for all of our series resources, visit: nwgospel.com/philippiansresources

HAVE A QUESTION?

---

[1] "Humility in Service," in The Valley of Vision, edited by Arthur Bennett (Edinburgh: Banner of Truth Trust, 1975), 326-327.

Philippians 2:19-30

GROUP DISCUSSION NOTES

PHILIPPIANS 3:1-11

Introduction

Imagine finally reaching the top of your career path. You pushed your way through all the "grunt work," been the "go-for," got the raises and promotions and worked your way up the ladder. At the top, you've finally gained the salary you've wanted. You've earned coveted recognition, have lead countless teams, and are now considered the expert of your field. However, the true "make or break" arrives when you're stuck between the choice of keeping your job or saving relationships with your loved ones. Do you take the money, the fame, and the recognition, or do you save your most significant relationships? Many have experienced this moment and have made their choice. Maybe it's not this specific moment, but you've likely faced a moment when you've had to ask yourself, "what am I willing to give up?"

As a Christian, this is a question that we are to ask every moment of following Christ. What are we willing to give up to have Christ? Paul declares that everything in our lives are nothing but rotting trash in comparison to the costly treasure it is to have Christ. In this passage, Paul warns against a group who are teaching that Jewish circumcision is a requirement for salvation. He emphasizes that no matter what qualifications or accomplishments he, or anyone else claims to have, nothing matters more than knowing Jesus! In the legalistic Jewish world of this time, Paul's qualifications mattered – they were everything. But Jesus flips that upside down. Instead of a list of qualifications, Paul wants Christians to pursue knowledge of and relationship with Jesus. However, this relationship with Jesus is far deeper than just knowledge, it includes walking the path that Jesus walked. This is the path of suffering, death, and resurrection. Through this all, Jesus grows and sanctifies His people, making them look more like Himself.

Philippians: That We May Know Him

What do we consider as "surpassing worth" in our lives? According to Paul, following Jesus not only involved giving up our self-earned "righteousness," but embracing a life of suffering, death, and resurrection. Is it worth it? Paul argues that knowing Jesus is the only thing of "surpassing worth." Is Jesus worth it to you?

PHILIPPIANS 3:1-11

Righteousness Through Faith in Christ

[1] Finally, my brothers, rejoice in the Lord. To write the same things to you is no trouble to me and is safe for you.

[2] Look out for the dogs, look out for the evildoers, look out for those who mutilate the flesh. [3] For we are the circumcision, who worship by the Spirit of God and glory in Christ Jesus and put no confidence in the flesh— [4] though I myself have reason for confidence in the flesh also. If anyone else thinks he has reason for confidence in the flesh, I have more: [5] circumcised on the eighth day, of the people of Israel, of the tribe of Benjamin, a Hebrew of Hebrews; as to the law, a Pharisee; [6] as to zeal, a persecutor of the church; as to righteousness under the law, blameless. [7] But whatever gain I had, I counted as loss for the sake of Christ. [8] Indeed, I count everything as loss because of the surpassing worth of knowing Christ Jesus my Lord. For his sake I have suffered the loss of all things and count them as rubbish, in order that I may gain Christ [9] and be found in him, not having a righteousness of my own that comes from the law, but that which comes through faith in Christ, the righteousness from God that depends on faith— [10] that I may know him and the power of his resurrection, and may share his sufferings, becoming like him in his death, [11] that by any means possible I may attain the resurrection from the dead.

Philippians: That We May Know Him

SERMON NOTES

Philippians 3:1-11

Philippians: That We May Know Him

DAY 1: ENGAGE THE TEXT

Read: Philippians 2:25-3:11 & Corinthians 2:1-5. In the context of last week's text, why should the Philippian Christians rejoice? What does a Christian consider as their greatest joy and treasure?

DAY 2: ENGAGE THE TEXT

Read: Philippians 3:2-3 & Romans 2:12-29. Paul asserts that physical circumcision no longer matters, but there is an analogy he uses. Beyond just the physical, what does it mean to be "spiritually circumcised?" What does it look like, in daily application, to worship by the Spirit, glory in Jesus, and have no confidence in the flesh?

Philippians: That We May Know Him

DAY 3: ENGAGE THE TEXT

Read: Philippians 3:4-6 & 2 Corinthians 11:16-33. Paul lists all that he, in the flesh, might find his righteousness in but chooses not to boast in. What are things that you are tempted to boast in? Take some time to pray, thanking God that you are made righteous through Christ alone.

DAY 4: ENGAGE THE TEXT

Read: Philippians 3:7-9 & Matthew 13:44-46. In the Kingdom of God, what is considered trash and what is considered treasure? How is this in conflict with our world? How would you describe knowing Christ in your own words?

Philippians: That We May Know Him

DAY 5: ENGAGE THE TEXT

Read: Philippians 3:10-11 and Romans 8:16-17. Jesus suffered on our behalf, a suffering that is beyond comprehension. What are some of the positive outcomes of Jesus' painful suffering? In comparison, looking at these texts of Scripture, what are some positive outcomes of our suffering in Christ?

Philippians 3:1-11

JOURNAL QUESTION

Throughout this text we see Paul determine that his own works and qualifications are nothing in comparison to the life that comes with knowing Christ. In what ways do you tend to trust in your own works or character? Write about that here in contrast to Christ's sufficiency. Think about how you can turn your focus from these things to knowing Jesus – which is far better!

Philippians: That We May Know Him

Philippians 3:1-11

GROUP DISCUSSION QUESTIONS

1. Why do you think that the clarification between legalism and salvation through Jesus alone is important to Paul? (verses 3-6)

2. In this passage, Paul discusses the legalism of those who believe circumcision is required for salvation (verses 2-6). What are some things that we tend to take pride in rather than resting in knowing Christ?

3. Paul counts everything as loss compared to the value of knowing Christ (verses 7-9). What is something that each of us could do to know Christ more closely?

4. How did Paul "share in Christ's sufferings? (verse 10)? How does the Church today do the same?

5. How does participating in suffering reveal the power of God? Have you experienced the power or presence of God in immense suffering?

GROUP ELEMENT

Pray together that each person in the group may be able to look not to their own merits but to the cross. Pray that each member of the group could grow in their knowledge of and relationship with Jesus! Each go around praying for the person to the right of them, that they would come to know and share in Jesus more closely.

HAVE A QUESTION?

Philippians 3:1-11

GROUP DISCUSSION NOTES

PHILIPPIANS 3:12-16

Introduction

Running for the health of it is one thing; running for first place is still another. However, we can look at this passage as one running for their very lives. People facing the fury of a huge storm in a disaster movie don't go back into their house for the heirloom dining set as the tidal wave approaches their city. They leave all possessions that would weigh them down for the chance at safety. Likewise, soldiers in war do not casually stroll across open spaces hoping that the other side has poor aim. They sprint towards their objective from cover to cover with nerves and senses alert to avoid a fatal shot. Surely, a man chased by wolves in the snowy mountains does not stop to number the jaws barking at his heels. No, he hoofs it with all possible haste towards shelter. The prize is life itself. Giving up the race is to accept death.

The children of God must run a similar race. We must withstand the Fall's tsunami of pain and brokenness. Satan shoots his fiery bolts to strike us down. The Old Self prowls in the dark jungles of our hearts, and it snaps at us with razor-sharp temptations. But, praise God, we have been transported to a fortress in Christ who protects us from death and places us on a path to eternal rest with Him. We need only continually hide His Word, which was with him in the beginning, in our hearts that we may know him and be known by him. In the arms of this Savior, we can run and not grow weary. By His strength we will run with Christ, but Jesus is the only one who will finally bring us to safety. He will carry you away from Death and into Life.

PHILIPPIANS 3:12-16

Straining Toward the Goal

[12] Not that I have already obtained this or am already perfect, but I press on to make it my own, because Christ Jesus has made me his own. [13] Brothers, I do not consider that I have made it my own. But one thing I do: forgetting what lies behind and straining forward to what lies ahead, [14] I press on toward the goal for the prize of the upward call of God in Christ Jesus. [15] Let those of us who are mature think this way, and if in anything you think otherwise, God will reveal that also to you. [16] Only let us hold true to what we have attained.

Philippians 3:12-16

SERMON NOTES

Philippians: That We May Know Him

Philippians 3:12-16

DAY 1: ENGAGE THE TEXT

Read: 2 Corinthians 4:1-6. In Philippians, Paul talks about how he is not yet perfect and his sanctification continues. How do his words in 2 Corinthians further outline how our sanctification comes about?

Philippians: That We May Know Him

DAY 2: ENGAGE THE TEXT

Read: 1 Corinthians 9:24-27. Paul often uses athletic metaphors to describe what it's like to follow Jesus. How does this passage help expand what Paul means to "press on?"

DAY 3: ENGAGE THE TEXT

Read: 1 Timothy 6:11-16. Once again, there is a unique partnership between the work of Christ in us and our work to live out our salvation. What does it look like to "take hold of eternal life?" What is the center of our hope in endurance?

Philippians: That We May Know Him

DAY 4: ENGAGE THE TEXT

Read: Hebrews 12:1-17. How does suffering impact our endurance? How does Hebrews further call us to endurance and give us hope?

DAY 5: ENGAGE THE TEXT

Read: Isaiah 35. What picture does the prophet paint of the life that is available for those who hope in God?

JOURNAL QUESTION

We've already seen how perspective really matters when it comes to our joy and our hope. After reading all the texts from this week, what is Jesus calling you to leave behind? What habits, activities, mindsets, or relationships do you need to let go of? When you cast your eyes to Christ, what has Jesus done for you and how does it motivate what you want to leave behind?

Philippians 3:12-16

Philippians: That We May Know Him

GROUP DISCUSSION QUESTIONS

1. Discuss what it means that Christ Jesus has made us his own (1:12). How then do we make Christ our own?

2. When Paul talks about the "prize of the upward call of God," what is he talking about? How has Christian culture sometimes misunderstood what the "prize" of eternity is?

3. How does this passage show us about how we grow in maturity? What is the mindset of a mature believer?

4. When are moments you find it hard to endure or to hold on tight to the truth? Where do moments of doubt and weariness sneak in?

5. How can lifting our eyes to Jesus change how we "press on?"

GROUP ELEMENT

In reference to this week's "Big Picture Journal Question;" take a moment to share things that Jesus is calling you to leave behind. Help each person brainstorm one tangible way they can remind themselves of the truth and to actively put away what they want to leave behind. Set a reminder on your phone to ask each other about it this week.

Philippians 3:12-16

HAVE A QUESTION?

GROUP DISCUSSION NOTES

PHILIPPIANS 3:17-4:1

Introduction

Where you're from can make a big difference. Preferences of food from the unique to the obscure can trace their roots back to a home town. The brands you shop for or the stores you go into vary from place to place. Even the way you say certain words depends on your "corner of the country." Do you pronounce "tour" as "tewer" or "tOR?" Do you call it a pill bug, potato bug, or rolly polly? Is it "kitty-corner" or "catty-corner?" Layer on cultures or countries of origin and the range of diversity continues to grow. Where you're a citizen can also make a huge difference depending on if you're a citizen in the country you stand in or not. No matter the country, being a citizen gives certain allowances that non-citizens do not have.

Multiple times in the New Testament, Paul refers to the Christian's citizenship in heaven. Those who are citizens of God's kingdom are welcomed into his family, given grace, and are united together with him. Citizens of the Kingdom of God have different, allegiances, live for a different purpose, and live differently than the citizens of the Kingdom of Darkness. Paul describes those in the Kingdom of Darkness as those who live in sin and unrepentance; they are enslaved to their appetites, celebrating shameful sin, and serving the things of the world. Unlike them, citizens of heaven may reside on earth but their allegiance is to God in heaven. This is the God who is sovereign over all things and in whom we eagerly await his return and redemption of our broken souls and bodies. Until that day, Paul encourages us to stand firm in our faith against the influences of the world remembering to whom we belong.

PHILIPPIANS 3:17-4:1

[17] Brothers, join in imitating me, and keep your eyes on those who walk according to the example you have in us. [18] For many, of whom I have often told you and now tell you even with tears, walk as enemies of the cross of Christ. [19] Their end is destruction, their god is their belly, and they glory in their shame, with minds set on earthly things. [20] But our citizenship is in heaven, and from it we await a Savior, the Lord Jesus Christ, [21] who will transform our lowly body to be like his glorious body, by the power that enables him even to subject all things to himself. [4:1] Therefore, my brothers, whom I love and long for, my joy and crown, stand firm thus in the Lord, my beloved

Philippians 3:17-4:1

SERMON NOTES

Philippians: That We May Know Him

Philippians 3:17-4:1

DAY 1: ENGAGE THE TEXT

Read: 1 Timothy 1:3-7, 18-20. In Philippians Paul talks about those who are enemies of the cross. How does his letter to Timothy show us how people first begin to swerve and then result in a shipwrecked faith?

DAY 2: ENGAGE THE TEXT

Read: Romans 8:1-11. How does Romans expand on what it means to have your mind set on earthly things and then to have a mind set on the Spirit? Where do you need to shift your mind from earthly things to spiritual things?

DAY 3: ENGAGE THE TEXT

Reflect on Philippians 3:19-20. Using Google, the Bible app, or a concordance, write out three verses that emphasize self-control. Identify a few areas of your life where you are struggling to fight your flesh and ask the Lord for help.

Philippians: That We May Know Him

DAY 4: ENGAGE THE TEXT

Read: Ephesians 2:19-22 & 1 Peter 2:9-12. What does it mean to be a citizens of heaven? What makes us into a citizen? What does a citizen look/act like?

_____
_____
_____
_____
_____
_____
_____
_____
_____
_____
_____
_____
_____
_____
_____
_____
_____
_____

DAY 5: ENGAGE THE TEXT

Read: 1 Corinthians 15:20-49. How does this passage show us Christ's supremacy over all things, and how does it bring clarity to what Paul says about our bodies being transformed to be like Christ's?

Philippians: That We May Know Him

JOURNAL QUESTION

Read: Acts 14:19; 2 Corinthians 11:24; & 2 Timothy 3:11. Contrast these verses with Philippians 3:18. Though Paul endured many hardships, what brings him to tears is reflecting on people living sinful and unrepentant lifestyles. How do you tend to respond to those around you who are living sinful and unrepentant lifestyles? This week, who can you make an intentional effort to pray for or connect with that is not walking with Christ?

Philippians 3:17-4:1

Philippians: That We May Know Him

GROUP DISCUSSION QUESTIONS

1. Jesus is our ultimate role model, but Paul encourages the Philippians to look to those who model Christ-likeness. When do you struggle to do this? Are there any worldly influences that you find challenging to ignore and tempting to follow?

2. Who do you look to for guidance in your relationship with Jesus? What qualities make them worth following?

3. When you think about people following your example as a Christian, how do you respond? Does it make you cringe, hesitate, or do you dodge it entirely?

4. What are areas of your life where you find yourself obliging the appetites of your flesh, or tend to have your mind set on earthly things?

5. Christians have a different 'citizenship.' How does knowing our allegiance is not to this world bring us comfort when we live different from the rest of the world?

6. Paul encourages people to "stand firm in the Lord." Examining your own life, where are you currently struggling to stand firm in the Lord? What is the cause? What can your community do to help you stand firm?

GROUP ELEMENT

One Sentence Popcorn Prayer: In this style of group prayer, you will take turns praying at random, but only speak a sentence at a time. Whether thanking the Lord for something, asking for help, or repenting, keep it short and sweet. There may be silence in between people speaking. Embrace this silence and listen to the Spirit. Before starting, select someone to wrap up the prayer when things naturally slow down.

Example:
Bob: "Jesus, thank you for placing these people in my life."
Susan: "Teach us to be patient."
Dave: "Use us in our community this week."

OTHER RESOURCES

In Drew Dyck's book titled, "Your Future Self Will Thank You: Secrets to Self-Control from the Bible and Brain Science (A Guide for Sinners, Quitters, and Procrastinators)" he brings out some helpful ways to think about self-control in our pursuit of obeying Jesus. You can see the link to his book as well as a link for a podcast interview with him from the Western Seminary produces podcast titled "Food Trucks in Babylon" at the resource page: nwgospel.com/philippiansresources

HAVE A QUESTION?

GROUP DISCUSSION NOTES

PHILIPPIANS 4:2-9
Introduction

Joy and peace often seem to be a package deal. Like inseparable friends, one is seldom seen without the other. In fact, they even start looking alike after a while. There they are, side by side, in Paul's list of spiritual fruit (Gal. 5:22), and, just as he suggests, they both wave invitingly to us from the lives of those we admire most.

But finding these companions for ourselves can pose a bit of a challenge. Stress, anxiety, and a host of insecurities seem to be more common companions to our daily lives. If Jesus made peace and joy available, as those Christmas angels promised, it seems logical that those of us who have chosen to follow Jesus would know how to lay hold of such traits. Sadly, though, many Christians live each day with little evidence of the peace or joy they're intended to enjoy.

In chapter 4 of Paul's letter to his friends at Philippi, the Apostle provides perhaps his clearest and most complete path to these wonderful gifts. This is the marvelous "end game" that the wisdom of this entire letter seeks. Initially, he addresses a conflict, an absence of peace, that may have been affecting many of his friends there. He doesn't explain their dividing issue, offer a solution, or referee their dispute. Instead, he calls them to a choice for peace, a choice motivated by a desire for unity above all other priorities.

Then, against this real-life backdrop, Paul unveils a path to the greater life that peace and joy portend. Choices—to rejoice, to be reasonable, to lay aside anxiety, and to pray with thanksgiving—offer peace as their destination, and surely joy can't be far behind. And what a peace it will be! Imagine peace that surpasses understanding, that doesn't depend on possessing every answer, or winning every battle. No wonder joy comes along too—and stays.

Philippians: That We May Know Him

If you want that peace and joy to remain, then Paul suggests that you refocus your thinking. Yeah, that's right—another choice. Rather than letting your day be darkened by all that sin can produce around you, let your thoughts be filled with greater things. Focus your heart and mind on truth, righteousness, and those things that can brighten your perspective. When you do, you'll find peace and have everything you need for joy.

PHILIPPIANS 4:2-9

Exhortation, Encouragement, and Prayer

² I entreat Euodia and I entreat Syntyche to agree in the Lord.
³ Yes, I ask you also, true companion, help these women, who have labored side by side with me in the gospel together with Clement and the rest of my fellow workers, whose names are in the book of life.

⁴ Rejoice in the Lord always; again I will say, rejoice. ⁵ Let your reasonableness be known to everyone. The Lord is at hand; ⁶ do not be anxious about anything, but in everything by prayer and supplication with thanksgiving let your requests be made known to God. ⁷ And the peace of God, which surpasses all understanding, will guard your hearts and your minds in Christ Jesus.

⁸ Finally, brothers, whatever is true, whatever is honorable, whatever is just, whatever is pure, whatever is lovely, whatever is commendable, if there is any excellence, if there is anything worthy of praise, think about these things. ⁹ What you have learned and received and heard and seen in me—practice these things, and the God of peace will be with you.

Philippians: That We May Know Him

SERMON NOTES

Philippians 4:2-9

Philippians: That We May Know Him

DAY 1: ENGAGE THE TEXT

In verse 2, Paul encourages Euodia and Syntyche to agree together. On what does Paul base this directive? How might such a directive impact your own moments of conflict with others?

Philippians 4:2-9

DAY 2: ENGAGE THE TEXT

Underline/circle how many times "rejoice" is used in this passage. What do you suppose it means to rejoice "in the Lord." How does knowing the incredible grace and hope of the gospel help you handle the more temporary frustrations and stresses of life?

Philippians: That We May Know Him

DAY 3: ENGAGE THE TEXT

One reason that Paul offers for being "reasonable" or "gentle" is that "the Lord is at hand." Likely, he doesn't mean this as a threat, but is calling the Philippians to make the gospel and the purposes of Christ's kingdom their greatest priority. What are some of the other priorities that can easily dominate your thinking? Do these other priorities provide or work against peace in your life?

DAY 4: ENGAGE THE TEXT

Why is thanksgiving such an important part of the praying that Paul encourages? How does remembering what God has already done for you strengthen your faith and trust in Him for the needs you are currently facing? Describe something God has done for you in the past that builds your faith each time you remember it.

Philippians: That We May Know Him

DAY 5: ENGAGE THE TEXT

Why can it be so difficult to focus on the kinds of things Paul wants us to think about in verse 8? Do you have friends that encourage you toward this kind of thinking? If so, write their names below and spend a few moments thanking God for such friends. If you have friends who steer your thoughts in other, less healthy, directions, what steps can you take to strengthen the peace and joy in your life?

Philippians 4:2-9

JOURNAL QUESTION

This week's text offers strong counsel toward several choices that will bring us closer to the life Christ desires for us. Which of Paul's directives would make the greatest impact in your life? What step(s) might help you make such a choice more consistently? What typically hinders you from making that choice?

Philippians: That We May Know Him

Philippians 4:2-9

GROUP DISCUSSION QUESTIONS

1. For Paul to include mention of the conflict he addresses in verse 2, the matter was likely affecting more than just those directly involved. How have the conflicts of others in the church impacted you or others and why?

2. What do we learn about Euodia and Syntyche in these verses and how does this information shape Paul's expectations for them? Do you think Paul would have the same expectations of us?

3. Which of the commands in verses 4-7 seem most challenging to you and why?

4. Is prayer an effective antidote to anxiety in your life? If so, in what way? If not, what keeps prayer from easing your worries?

5. What prevents us from focusing our thoughts on those things Paul lists in verse 8? How might the steps listed in verses 4-7 help us to choose the thoughts described in verse 8?

6. What impact do you think Paul's example (vs 9) in these matters had on the Philippians? Whose example of a life of peace and joy has impacted you?

GROUP ELEMENT

Return to Group Discussion question 3 and encourage each group member to respond. Spend a few moments praying for one other. Invite those who are willing to lead the group in praying for one or more of their friends.

As you close the group meeting, ask group members to share at least one answer to prayer or way in which God has impacted their lives. Include expressions of thankfulness as you also pray for the current needs of the group.

HAVE A QUESTION?

Philippians 4:2-9

GROUP DISCUSSION NOTES

PHILIPPIANS 4:10-13
Introduction

Philippians 4:13 is a verse many of us can likely recite from memory. It is typically heard in the context of a sports game won, written in an Instagram bio, or given as an encouragement for a promotion at work. Does this verse mean we can succeed in every desire we may have? Within the context of this passage, written by Paul from prison, we see what it truly means to do all things through Christ who brings true contentment. He doesn't say that he has found the secret to having everything turn out the way he wants. He declares that even in great need he abounds because he has Christ. This is the secret to contentment.

Throughout Philippians 4:10-13, Paul discusses the way that the Lord has provided for him in times of need, both through the church in Philippi and through His nearness. In verse 10, readers see Paul discussing how the church's concern for him has been revived as they had an opportunity to care for him. He continues to discuss throughout the later three verses how the Lord has provided for him by bringing him the contentment that is only found in Jesus!

We may not currently find ourselves in a similar situation to Paul (arrested for sharing the gospel) but we all know the trials and temptations that life in our world can bring. Like Paul, let us learn to cast our eyes to Jesus to whom all our joy and contentment can be found.

PHILIPPIANS 4:10-13

God's Provision

[10] I rejoiced in the Lord greatly that now at length you have revived your concern for me. You were indeed concerned for me, but you had no opportunity. [11] Not that I am speaking of being in need, for I have learned in whatever situation I am to be content. [12] I know how to be brought low, and I know how to abound. In any and every circumstance, I have learned the secret of facing plenty and hunger, abundance and need. [13] I can do all things through him who strengthens me.

Philippians 4:10-13

SERMON NOTES

Philippians: That We May Know Him

Philippians 4:10-13

DAY 1: ENGAGE THE TEXT

Read: Philippians 4:10 & Philippians 4:16-18. With verses 16-18 in view, what way do you think the Philippian Christians showed their concern for Paul? How do you respond to this? How do you tend to express concern for the Church and for Christian leaders in need?

Philippians: That We May Know Him

DAY 2: ENGAGE THE TEXT

Read: Philippians 4:11; Acts 14:19; & reread Acts 16:19-24. Knowing what these texts say, what are the specific circumstances in which Paul had to be content? What about Paul's response of contentment stands out to you?

Philippians 4:10-13

DAY 3: ENGAGE THE TEXT

Read: Philippians 4:12 & Psalm 73:26-28. Paul states here that he can be content in any circumstance, good or bad. Why do you think that is? Reflecting on the Psalm 73 passage, what words does the Psalmist use to describe God? How do these two passages connect?

Philippians: That We May Know Him

DAY 4: ENGAGE THE TEXT

Read: Philippians 4:13 & 2 Corinthians 12:7-10. In the last verse of this weeks' passage Paul gives readers the secret to contentment. How does the 2 Corinthians passage elaborate on this? How are we strong in our struggles?

_____
_____
_____
_____
_____
_____
_____
_____
_____
_____
_____
_____
_____
_____
_____
_____
_____
_____

DAY 5: ENGAGE THE TEXT

Read: Philippians 4:11-13 & Romans 8:31-39. How can Paul be content in what he knows about God as discussed in the Romans 8 passage? How do these truths and attributes of God bring contentment to you in your trials?

Philippians: That We May Know Him

JOURNAL QUESTION

Throughout this passage we have seen Paul rejoice in God's provision both through His people and through Jesus being his strength. What seasons, struggles, or trials have you experienced throughout your life and more recently? Have you struggled to be content in Christ or has that come easily to you? How can you grow in that? Pray that the Lord would help you to rejoice in His provision and be content in Him.

Philippians 4:10-13

GROUP DISCUSSION QUESTIONS

1. In verse 10, Paul speaks of the opportunity that the believers in Philippi had to show their concern for him. How can believers today look for opportunities to express their concern for their Christian leaders, brothers, and sisters both locally and around the world?

2. Verse 11 discusses contentment regardless of what situation one is in. Does contentment come naturally or is it difficult for you?

3. Last week, we discussed the importance of thanksgiving which makes contentment come much more naturally. What attributes of God, who is unchanging, are you thankful for?

4. In times of trial, what do you forget about God? How can we encourage one another in these truths?

5. How does your mindset shift when you are brought low compared to when you abound? How does that reveal our source of hope?

6. Verse 13 is often taken out of context and misinterpreted in our culture. In view of the first three verses in this passage, what does it mean to do all things through Him who strengthens us? How can we rest in Christ working through us in our trials?

Philippians 4:10-13

GROUP ELEMENT

Give an opportunity for everyone to share a trial that they or a loved one are going through. Pray together that they would all find contentment in Christ throughout their trials. If applicable, brainstorm ways that everyone can support one another in trials whether with prayer, encouraging words, or providing for practical needs.

OTHER RESOURCES

Read the article titled "Victory Through Suffering: The True Meaning of Philippians 4:13" by The Gospel Coalition and other resources at our resource page: nwgospel.com/philippiansresources.

HAVE A QUESTION?

Philippians: That We May Know Him

GROUP DISCUSSION NOTES

PHILIPPIANS 4:14-23
Introduction

You've got a friend in me
You've got a friend in me
When the road looks rough ahead
And you're miles and miles
From your nice warm bed
You just remember what your old pal said
Boy, you've got a friend in me
Yeah, you've got a friend in me

Made popular in Toy Story, "You've Got a Friend in Me" by Randy Newman resonates with just about everyone. Who doesn't value a genuine friendship and the comfort of knowing that, somewhere out there, you've got someone on your side who is going to have your back.

The Apostle Paul closes his letter to the Philippians by reminding them of the incredible role that they have played in his ministry. They shared in Paul's troubles (v. 14). They partnered with Paul when other churches ignored and rejected him (v. 15). They supported Paul and met his needs as he labored in the work of evangelism and church planting (v. 16). Paul has a dear friend in the church of Philippi, and he's bold in his articulation of his appreciation.

By his grace and according to his own design, God has determined that one of the primary means for the sending, supporting, and sustaining of gospel workers is the Church. In part, 'to be the Church' means to support the work of gospel ministry, to partner with gospel laborers, and to be an agent of encouragement for those putting their hands to the plow of evangelism and church planting. God is exceedingly gracious for calling every Christian to plan a part in this most glorious of tasks.

PHILIPPIANS 4:14-23

[14] Yet it was kind of you to share my trouble. [15] And you Philippians yourselves know that in the beginning of the gospel, when I left Macedonia, no church entered into partnership with me in giving and receiving, except you only. [16] Even in Thessalonica you sent me help for my needs once and again. [17] Not that I seek the gift, but I seek the fruit that increases to your credit. [18] I have received full payment, and more. I am well supplied, having received from Epaphroditus the gifts you sent, a fragrant offering, a sacrifice acceptable and pleasing to God. [19] And my God will supply every need of yours according to his riches in glory in Christ Jesus. [20] To our God and Father be glory forever and ever. Amen.

Final Greetings
[21] Greet every saint in Christ Jesus. The brothers who are with me greet you. [22] All the saints greet you, especially those of Caesar's household.

[23] The grace of the Lord Jesus Christ be with your spirit.

Philippians 4:14-23

SERMON NOTES

Philippians: That We May Know Him

DAY 1: ENGAGE THE TEXT

What is so significant about what the Philippians offered Paul? How did they support Paul's ministry?

Philippians: That We May Know Him

DAY 2: ENGAGE THE TEXT

What does Paul mean when he says that he didn't seek "the gift" while seeking "the fruit that increases to [the Philippians' credit]" (Philippians 4:17)? What does this teach you about the nature of gospel ministry?

DAY 3: ENGAGE THE TEXT

Read: 2 Corinthians 8:1-15. What does this passage teach you about how Christians ought to support the work of gospel ministry?

Philippians: That We May Know Him

DAY 4: ENGAGE THE TEXT

What does this passage teach you about how God works in and through his people?

Philippians 4:14-23

DAY 5: ENGAGE THE TEXT

"All the saints greet you, especially those of Caesar's household" (Philippians 4:22). What is so significant about this statement from the Apostle Paul? What does this teach you about how the power and spread of the gospel?

Philippians: That We May Know Him

JOURNAL QUESTION

What does it mean to support the work of gospel ministry? Where do you see gospel ministry taking place, and how has God specially placed and equipped you to be an agent of encouragement and support for this work?

Philippians 4:14-23

GROUP DISCUSSION QUESTIONS

1. What does it look like for Christians to "share in [the] trouble" (v. 14) of cross-cultural missionaries and church planters? Similarly, what does "partnership" (v. 15) in gospel ministry look like?

2. To what end should you follow in the example of the Philippians? How does imitating them ultimately glorify Christ?

3. What is the fruit of gospel ministry? What does it mean to share in that fruit?

4. How does Paul describe the gift sent to him from the Philippians and delivered by Epaphroditus? What does this teach you about how God views your support of gospel ministry?

5. What assurance is there in this passage? What has God guaranteed his people in their support of his work?

GROUP ELEMENT

Take time as a group to make a list of different gospel workers (missionaries, pastors/elders, missions organizations, etc.) and pray for God's providence in their work.

OTHER RESOURCES

Northwest Gospel Church partners with a network of church planting churches who work together to see the church grow all around the world. To learn more about this network you can find a link to the Acts29 page as well as our other resources at nwgospel.com/philippiansresources

HAVE A QUESTION?

Philippians: That We May Know Him

GROUP DISCUSSION NOTES

CLOSING REFLECTION

Over the last twelve weeks (that's 3 months!), we have slowed down to really dive into the letter of Philippians. Over that time we have been confronted with the ways that often doubt God, look to other things for our contentment, and have recognized areas of grumbling in our heart. We have also seen a beautiful picture of Jesus. The one who was God, equal in glory, and yet took on the humble form of a human to die a criminals death. Jesus humility has redeemed us all and has become the name to whom all creation will worship. It because of Jesus that we pursue godliness and unity with God's people.

Take some time here at the end of this series to flip back over this book and the lessons you have worked through. Then do your best here to summarize what the Lord would have you take away from this time together and from his word.

Philippians: That We May Know Him

Closing Reflection

Philippians: That We May Know Him

SCRIPTURE REFERENCES

WEEK 1:
Philippians 1:1-11
Acts 16:1-15
Acts 16:16-40
1 Thessalonians 5:2–11
2 Peter 3:10–13
Revelation 20:11–21:8

WEEK 2:
Philippians 1:12-18a
Acts 16:25-24
James 2:2
Acts 4:23-31
Acts 28:30-31
2 Corinthians 11:1-15

WEEK 3:
Philippians 1:18b-30
Romans 1:1-16
Galatians 2:20
Romans 15:1-7
Ephesians 4:1-6
1 Peter 4:12-19

WEEK 4:
Philippians 2:1-11
Colossians 3:1-17
Colossians 1:15-20
John 1:1-4
Romans 12:9-21
Isaiah 42:1-9
Revelation 5

WEEK 5:
Philippians 2:12-18
Hebrews 13
1 Peter 2:13-24
Matthew 5:1-16
John 8:12-30
John 6:60-71
Matthew 28:19-20
1 John 5:1-5

WEEK 6: Philippians 2:19-30
2 Timothy 1:1-14
1 Timothy 3:1-13
Ephesians 6:21-24
Colossians 4:7-18
1 Thessalonians 5:12-28

WEEK 7: Philippians 3:1-11
1 Corinthians 2:1-5
Romans 2:12-29
2 Corinthians 11:16-33
Matthew 13:44-46
Romans 8:16-17

WEEK 8: Philippians 3:12-16
2 Corinthians 4:1-6
1 Corinthians 9:24-27
1 Timothy 6:11-16
Hebrews 12:1-17
Isaiah 35

WEEK 9:
Philippians 3:17-4:1
1 Timothy 1:3-7
1 Timothy 1:18-20
Romans 8:1-11
Ephesians 2:19-22
1 Peter 2:9-12
1 Corinthians 15:20-49
Acts 14:19;
2 Corinthians 11:24
2 Timothy 3:11

WEEK 10:
Philippians 4:2-9

WEEK 11:
Philippians 4:10-13
Psalm 73:26-28
Acts 14:19
Acts 16:19-24
2 Corinthians 12:7-10
Romans 8:31-39

WEEK 12:
Philippians 4:14-23
2 Corinthians 8:1-15

Made in the USA
Columbia, SC
15 August 2023